AF173234

PUPIL'S BOOK 4

Contents

Welcome

1 🎧 1:02 Talk about the pictures. Then listen and read.

1

IT IS NIGHT ON ICE ISLAND. HECTOR FROST IS AT HOME.

Smith!

2

My diamonds and I...

Ah, those beautiful diamonds! I want those diamonds, Smith.

Yes, boss.

Yap!

SMITH IS TAKING THE DIAMONDS.

3

Where are the Queen's diamonds, Smith?

They're in the town, boss.

Not for long. Ha, ha, ha!

4

Classy!

5

Ha, ha! Well done, Smith! They're MY diamonds now!

Yes, boss.

BANG

6

What was THAT?

BANG

2 Act out the story.

3

1 Friends

1 What do you know?

2  Listen and read. Who lives at number twelve?

3 Listen and say.

good-looking

spiky hair

straight hair

bald

handsome

beautiful

cute

4  Talk about your friends.

Lily's got straight hair.

Arthur's good-looking.

Can identify people and what they look like

5 Listen and read. Then look and say.

1   She's got blond hair and blue eyes.
2   He's got spiky hair and brown eyes.
3   She's got straight hair and glasses.
4   He's got brown hair and green eyes.
5   They've got brown hair.

 Maddy
 Emma
 Robbie
 Dan

6 Ask and answer. *True* or *false*?

A: What does Maddy look like?
B: She's got dark hair.
A: False. She's got light hair.

7 Play the game.

A: He, she or they?
B: He.
A: What does he look like?
B: He's got long hair and a beard.
    He hasn't got a moustache.
A: He's number two.

LOOK!
1:07

| What **does** he/she **look like**? | She**'s** beautiful. She**'s got** blond hair. |
| What **do** they **look like**? | They**'re** tall. They**'ve got** brown hair. |

bald   beard   beautiful   curly   cute   fat   glasses
good-looking   handsome   long   moustache   old
pretty   short   spiky   straight   thin   ugly   young

8 Listen and say.

SONG

1 — "Get up now!" — bossy

2 — sporty

3 — lazy

4 — shy

5 — kind

6 — clever

9 Listen, read and sing.

You've got me
And I've got you.
You help, you listen
And I do, too.
We're friends. We're friends.

You're lazy at home.
You're shy at school.
But you're sporty and clever
And very cool.
We're friends. We're friends.

You're sometimes bossy
But I don't mind.
I like you
Because you're kind.
We're friends. We're friends.
We're friends. We're friends.

LOOK!

You're sporty **and** you're clever.

You're bossy **but** I don't mind.

I like you **because** you're kind.

10 Read and choose.

1 She's sporty (but / because) she isn't very clever.
2 We don't like Tom (but / because) he's very bossy.
3 They've got brown hair (and / but) brown eyes.
4 She's clever (but / because) she's lazy at school.
5 He hasn't got a lot of friends (but / because) he's very shy.

11 Talk about people in your family.

- mum
- sister
- granny
- dad
- brother
- grandad

I like my granny because she isn't bossy. She's funny and kind.

Can use adjectives to describe what a person is like

12 Look and read. What are the names of the children in the Torres family?

The Torres family

Seb

From: seb@yoohoo.com
To: matt@gogomail.com
Subject: Spain!

Hi Matt,

I'm having a great time here in Spain. I'm staying with the Torres family this summer. They've got a beautiful home in Madrid.

Carlos is twelve. He's shy but he's very kind. He's clever, too. My Spanish isn't very good but he speaks great English. He's got a granny in Los Angeles and she speaks English with Carlos.

He's got two sisters, Nerea and Lucía. Nerea is fifteen. She's got beautiful brown hair and she's very sporty. She isn't at home this week because she's got a big tennis competition. Lucía is nine. She's funny but she's very bossy. She wants to play games all the time!

See you soon,

Seb

13  Read and say. *True* or *false*?

1 Seb is in Spain.
2 Seb has got a new home.
3 Carlos is clever.
4 Nerea likes sport.
5 Carlos has got a lazy sister.

14 Act out the dialogue between Seb and his mum.

Seb's mum:

• Are you having a good time?
• Is Carlos nice?
• What does he look like?
• Has he got a brother or sister?
• What do they look like?

SOUNDS FUN!

15 1:13 Listen, read and say.

My friend's very pretty.
She's sporty but shy.
She likes funny glasses.
I don't know why!

1 ICE PALACE

Oh, no, I can't see the skidoo now.

Come on, let's get some ice cream and make a plan.

2 PALACE

I love strawberry ice cream.

Poor Gizmo.

3 INSIDE THE ICE PALACE

What do the thieves look like?

I think one's got spiky hair and the other has got straight hair.

4

Have they got beards?

Are they tall or short?

I don't know.

5

Huh?!

WOOF!

What is it, Gizmo?

6

It's the man from the skidoo! And he hasn't got hair.

Follow him, quick!

Rrrrruff!

17  Act out the story.

19 **Look and read. Do you like the pictures? Why?**

A

This picture is by Auguste Renoir, an artist from France (1841 to 1919). It is in warm colours.

B

This picture is by Vincent van Gogh, an artist from the Netherlands (1853 to 1890). It is in cool colours.

20  **Read, look and say.**

It's Picture A!

1 This picture's got a lot of yellow and red.
2 This picture's got a lot of green and white.
3 This picture's got cool colours.
4 This picture's got warm colours.

MINI PROJECT

22 **Write about a painting.**

- **Think** of a painting you like.
- **Plan** by making notes about the painting. Are the colours in the painting warm or cool? How do they make you feel?
- **Write** five sentences about the painting.
- **Share** what you have learnt about the painting.

21 **Imagine and answer the questions. Then share with a friend.**

1 What time of day is it in Picture A?
2 How do the girls in Picture A feel?
3 How does Picture A make you feel?
4 How does Picture B make you feel?

HOME SCHOOL LINK

Listen and number.

24 **Circle. Then ask and answer.**

1 **A:** What does her sister look like? / What do they look like?
   B: They've got straight hair and glasses.
2 **A:** What does your mum look like? / What does your brother look like?
   B: He's got spiky hair and brown eyes.
3 **A:** What does your dad look like? / What does Sally look like?
   B: She's got straight hair but she hasn't got blue eyes. She's got brown eyes!

25 **Write. Then ask and answer.**

1 Is your best friend clever? _____
2 What does your mum look like? _____
3 Is your dad sporty and handsome? _____
4 Are you shy? _____
5 What do you look like? _____

I can ask and answer questions about what people look like.
I can talk about the personalities of my friends and family.
I can write about a painting and its colours.

26 **Create a new character.**

1 Circle.

My new character is...

thin fat ugly
handsome happy
beautiful bald
sporty
clever short
good-looking tall

2 Write.

My new character's got... (thin, long, short, pink, etc.)

_____ _____ hair

a _____ body   _____ legs
a _____ head   _____ arms
a _____ face   _____ eyes
a _____ mouth   _____ ears

3 Draw. Then tell a friend.

4 Listen to your friend. Draw his/her new character.

5 Tell the class about your character. What is it like? What does it look like?

27 **I want to know more!**

My new character is tall and handsome. He's got short spiky hair and green eyes. He's bossy but clever. He likes surfing.

Now go to Poptropica English World

Wider World 1
Families of the world

1  **What do you know?**

2 🎧 1:22 **Listen and read. Are the families big or small?**

3 **Number the photos.**

1 ●●●
Kyle's blog

In the United Kingdom, some families are big and some are small. My family is very big now. My mum's got a new husband. He helps me with my homework. He's got a son, so now I've got a brother. We play football together every Saturday. We have fun!

Kyle, 12, United Kingdom

2 ●●●
Lang's blog

A lot of families here in China have got only one child. I haven't got a brother or sister but I'm not sad. I live with my mum, dad, granny and grandad. My grandparents play games with me. They're very clever and sporty! I love my small family.

Lang, 11, China

Can understand texts about families around the world

c

3

James's blog

I live in the United States. Big families are great! My friends have got small families but I have got a mum and dad, three sisters and three brothers. In my family, the big children help the small children. My sister, Jill, is 17 and she helps me with my homework. She's bossy but she's kind, too.

James, 12, United States

5  **Ask and answer.**

1   How big is your family?
2   Are families in your country big or small?

4  **Read again and say.**
True or *false*?

1   James likes his big family.
2   Lang is happy.
3   Lang plays games with her sisters.
4   In Britain, all families are small.
5   Kyle likes his new brother.

YOUR TURN!

What is good and bad about big and small families? Discuss in pairs. Then tell the class.

	Good	Bad
Small family	more time with parents	no brothers or sisters to play with
Big family		

My life

1 **What do you know?**

2 1:23 **Listen and read. Is Kipper a good cat?**

1 After school, Maddy meets her friends.

Go away, Kipper!

2 In the afternoon, Emma and Dan do their homework. Maddy and Robbie play computer games.

Oh, no! Our homework.

Go away, Kipper!

3 In the evening, Maddy brushes her teeth. Kipper wants to brush his teeth, too.

GO AWAY, Kipper!

4 Before bed, Maddy does her homework.

Your Pet
How long is
his tail?

Oh, no. My homework is about Kipper. Kipper, where are you?

3  1:24 **Listen and say.**

1  brush my teeth

2  make my bed

3  wash my face

4  tidy my room

5  do my homework

6  meet my friends

7  be on time

8  take notes in class

4  1:25 **Listen and play the memory game.**

Can identify daily activities and routines

5   Listen, look and say.

What do we do before bed?

1 ❓ brush their hair.
2 ❓ washes its head.
3 ❓ washes her face.
4 ❓ brush our teeth.
5 ❓ does his homework.

the bird

Dan

Mum and Dad

LOOK!

1:28

He does **his** homework.
She washes **her** face.
It washes **its** head.
We brush **our** teeth.
They brush **their** hair.

Emma and I

Maddy

6 Look and say.

Maddy makes her bed at half past eight.

1 Maddy / make her bed / at half past eight.
2 My family and I / brush our teeth / in the morning.
3 Robbie and Emma / meet their friends / at four o'clock.
4 My brother / do his homework / in the evening.
5 Our cat / wash its face / every day.

Three... six... five. She does her homework at half past eleven.

7 Play the game. Spin, look and say.

	Spin 1	Spin 2	Spin 3
1	I	wash/hair	6.00
2	They	brush/teeth	7.30
3	She	meet/friends	9.00
4	It	tidy/room	2.30
5	We	take notes/in class	11.30
6	He	do/homework	10.00

8   **Listen and sing.**

1:31
1:32

1:33

my sister**'s** kite
a monster**'s** head
my brother**'s** ball

I always wash my face before school
But I never brush my hair so I look cool.
I usually make my bed
And I sometimes help my mum.
But I never, never tidy my room.
Never, never tidy my room.

My brother tidies his room.
My sister tidies her room.
My friends tidy their rooms
But not me! Oh, no! Not me!
I never, never tidy my room.
Never, never tidy my room.

Where's my sister's kite? Is it under the bed?
And on the chair, what's that? A monster's head!
My brother's ball is here, too.
But where is it? Well, I don't know.
Because I never, never tidy my room.
Never, never tidy my room.
Never, never tidy my room.

9 **Look and say. What colour is it?**

> Matt's bed is blue.

> Matt's bed   Matt's chair   his brother's ball
> his sister's kite   the monster's head

10 **Listen and repeat. Then listen, look and say.**

1:34

> always   usually   often   sometimes   never

> Sasha always brushes
> her teeth.

Sasha's week	Monday	Tuesday	Wednesday	Thursday	Friday	Saturday	Sunday
brush her teeth	■	■	■	■	■	■	■
make her bed	■			■	■		■
do her homework	■	■	■		■	■	■
help with dinner							
tidy her room	■		■				

Can use always / usually / often / sometimes / never

11 1:35 **Listen and circle. What is Peter's score?**

QUIZ! ARE YOU A **M☉RNING** PERSON?

Some people like mornings. What about you?

1 Do you get up on time in the morning?
1 No, never.
2 Yes, sometimes.
3 Yes, often.
4 Yes, usually.
5 Yes, always.

2 Do you have a big breakfast?
1 No, never.
2 Yes, sometimes.
3 Yes, often.
4 Yes, usually.
5 Yes, always.

3 Do you talk to your friends and family before school?
1 No, never.
2 Yes, sometimes.
3 Yes, often.
4 Yes, usually.
5 Yes, always.

4 Do you make your bed in the morning?
1 No, never.
2 Yes, sometimes.
3 Yes, often.
4 Yes, usually.
5 Yes, always.

5 Do you make your family's breakfast?
1 No, never.
2 Yes, sometimes.
3 Yes, often.
4 Yes, usually.
5 Yes, always.

6 Do you get to school on time?
1 No, never.
2 Yes, sometimes.
3 Yes, often.
4 Yes, usually.
5 Yes, always.

YOUR SCORE!

6–14 The morning is a bad time of day for you. Maybe you're an afternoon person!

15–22 You're OK in the morning but not great.

23–30 Wow! You're a fantastic morning person!

12  **Look at Activity 11 and talk about Peter's day. Then quiz your partner. Is he/she a morning person?**

I always get up on time in the morning.

13  1:36 **Listen and circle.**

1 Emma (is / isn't) a morning person.
2 Emma (always / sometimes) makes her bed in the morning.
3 Emma (sometimes / never) has a small breakfast.
4 Emma (never / often) helps in the kitchen in the morning.
5 Emma (likes / doesn't like) talking in the morning.

SOUNDS FUN!

14 1:37 **Listen, read and say.**

She goes home and does her homework.
She washes her hair and nose.
But she never brushes her toes.

15   **Talk about the pictures. Then listen and read.**
1:40

1. What's this place?
   It's the training camp.

2. Let's hide.
   Hey, look at this! We can build an igloo.

3. He's keeping fit.
   Phew. Look at that! He's one strong guy!
   Rrrong!

4. Mmm. It's nice and warm here.
   Hey, come on. Watch the man. Stay awake, Polly.
   YAWN

5. SOME TIME LATER...
   Oh, no, he isn't here! We can't catch him now.
   What's that?

6. It's his shopping.
   And these ribbons are like the ribbons in the newspaper! Yes!
   Rrres!

16   **Act out the story.**

Can understand a simple story / Can discuss a story

17 What do you know?

18 Read. Is Jonas healthy?
1:41

Jonas is a football player. He plays football every day. Pasta is his favourite food. He's very healthy because he eats a lot of fruit. He's got strong bones, too because he likes drinking milk. He always brushes his teeth after breakfast and again before bed. He doesn't go to the doctor or dentist very often.

HEALTHY MENU FOR TUESDAY

★ **BREAKFAST** ★
Cereal with milk
Toast
A banana
Orange juice

LUNCH
Chicken pasta with green salad
An orange
Water

DINNER
Vegetable soup and bread
Fish, potatoes and carrots
Apple pie
Milk

19 Read again and say.

1 Jonas likes playing ?.
2 Jonas's favourite food is ?.
3 In the morning, he always brushes his ?.
4 Jonas likes drinking ?.

20 Read and find.

1 Apples and bananas are examples of this.
2 These are white and in every part of your body.
3 This is a white drink. It is good for your bones.
4 Have you got bad teeth? See this person.
5 This is a drink made from fruit.
6 This is an orange vegetable.

MINI PROJECT

21 Make a menu.

- **Think** about what foods are healthy and what foods are bad for your teeth.
- **Plan** a menu with three healthy meals.
- **Write** your menu.
- **Share** your menu with your friends and try it at home.

HOME SCHOOL LINK

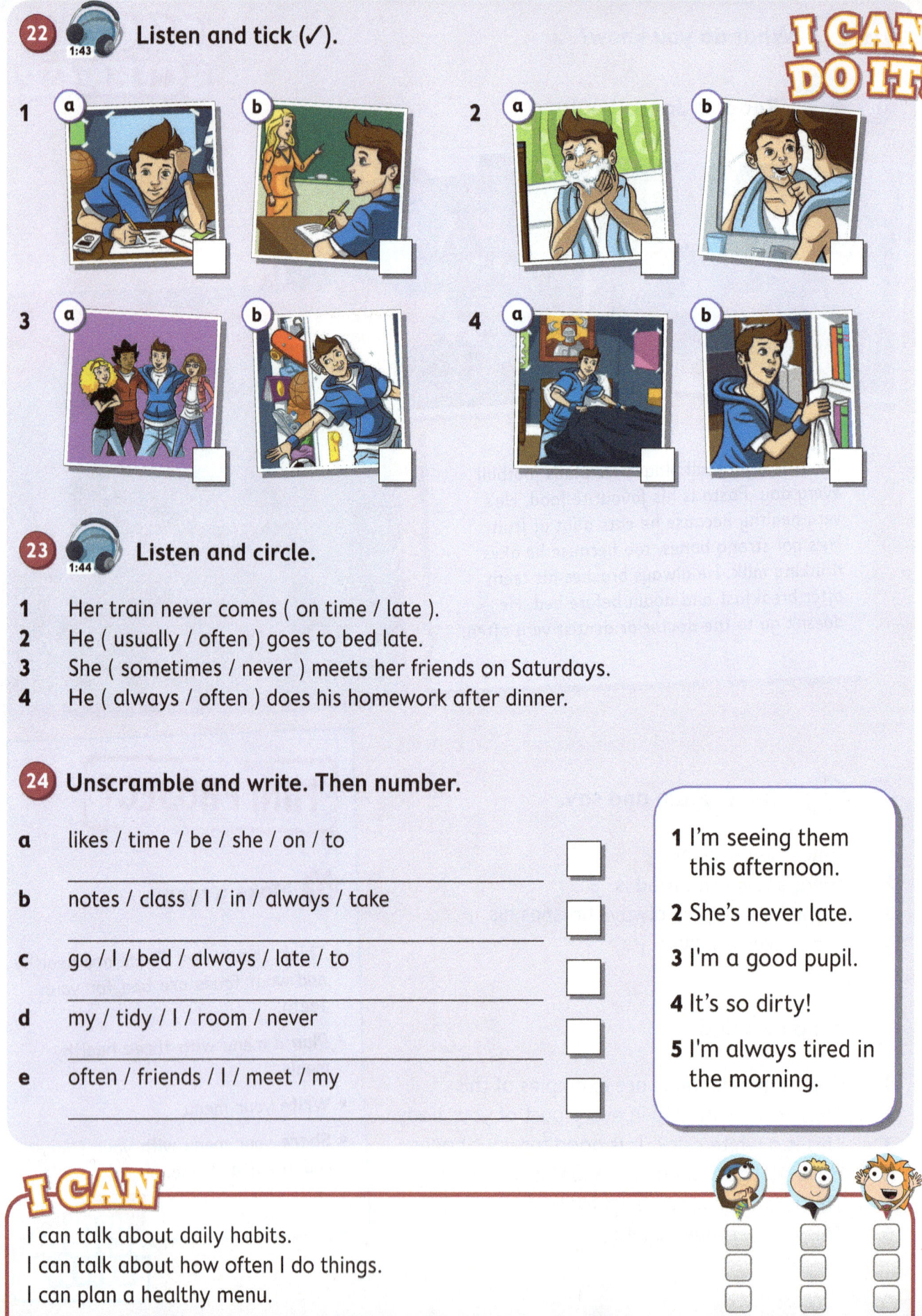

22 1:43 **Listen and tick (✓).**

1 a b   2 a b

3 a b   4 a b

23 1:44 **Listen and circle.**

1 Her train never comes (on time / late).
2 He (usually / often) goes to bed late.
3 She (sometimes / never) meets her friends on Saturdays.
4 He (always / often) does his homework after dinner.

24 Unscramble and write. Then number.

a likes / time / be / she / on / to

_____

b notes / class / I / in / always / take

_____

c go / I / bed / always / late / to

_____

d my / tidy / I / room / never

_____

e often / friends / I / meet / my

_____

1 I'm seeing them this afternoon.

2 She's never late.

3 I'm a good pupil.

4 It's so dirty!

5 I'm always tired in the morning.

I CAN

I can talk about daily habits.
I can talk about how often I do things.
I can plan a healthy menu.

Can assess what I have learnt in Unit 2

Sue

Alex

Alice

Max

1 Choose a person. What is he/she like?

2 Is he/she healthy?

3 What does he/she eat for breakfast?

4 Write about his/her week.

(Sue / Alex / Alice / Max) always _____.

He/She usually _____.

_____ often _____.

_____ sometimes _____.

_____ never _____.

5 Find someone who chose the same person. Compare.

Alex is clever and sporty. He eats two eggs with toast and fruit for breakfast. He always brushes his teeth after eating.

I think Alex is kind and shy. He has juice, yoghurt and an apple for breakfast. He is never late for work.

26 **I want to know more!**

Now go to Poptropica English World

3 Free time

1 ⭐ What do you know?

2 🎧 1:46 Listen and read. Is Robbie good at throwing?

3 🎧 1:47 Listen and say.

hitting

throwing

climbing

diving

kicking

catching

running races

4 🎧 1:48 Listen, think and say.

Can talk about free-time activities

5 🎧 1:50 **Listen and read. Then look and match.**

1   She's good at diving.
2   He's good at throwing.
3   She isn't good at dancing.
4   They aren't good at climbing.
5   He isn't good at hitting.
6   They're good at riding.

🎧 1:51 **LOOK!**

I**'m good at** throw**ing**.
You**'re good at** kick**ing**.
She **isn't good at** danc**ing**.
They **aren't good at** climb**ing**.

6 🌐 **Cover the sentences in Activity 5. Look and say.**

A: Picture d.
B: He's good at throwing.

7 🌐 **Play the game.**

Diving!

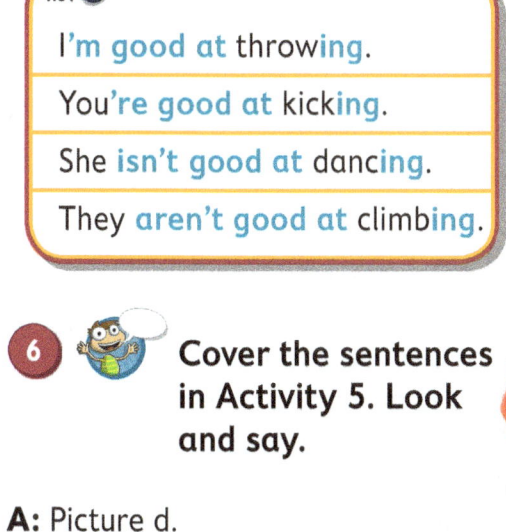

8 🎧 1:53 **Listen and say.**

SONG

1
drawing

2
rollerblading

3
trampolining

Chorus:
Come and have fun at the Fun Club.
Come here and meet new friends.
Drawing, trampolining, rollerblading,
At the Fun Club, the fun never ends.

What do you like doing?
Do you like playing the drums?
Or skateboarding or acting?
There's fun for everyone.

What are you good at?
Are you good at playing chess?
We love Fun Club!
It's fun here. Yes! Yes! Yes!

Chorus

4
playing chess

5
acting

6
skateboarding

7
playing the drums

9 🎧 1:54 1:55 **Listen, read and sing.**

10 💬 **Find and say.**

Emma loves rollerblading.

Emma   Dan   Maddy

LOOK!
🎧 1:56

What do you **like** do**ing**?

What **are** you **good at**?

He/She **loves** skateboard**ing**.

They **like** act**ing**.

11 💬 **Ask and answer.**

A: What are you good at?
B: I'm good at playing chess.
A: What do you like doing?
B: I like trampolining but I don't like rollerblading.

Can identify more free-time activities and hobbies

12  1:58 **Listen, think and choose.**

Hettie   Cosmo   Fred

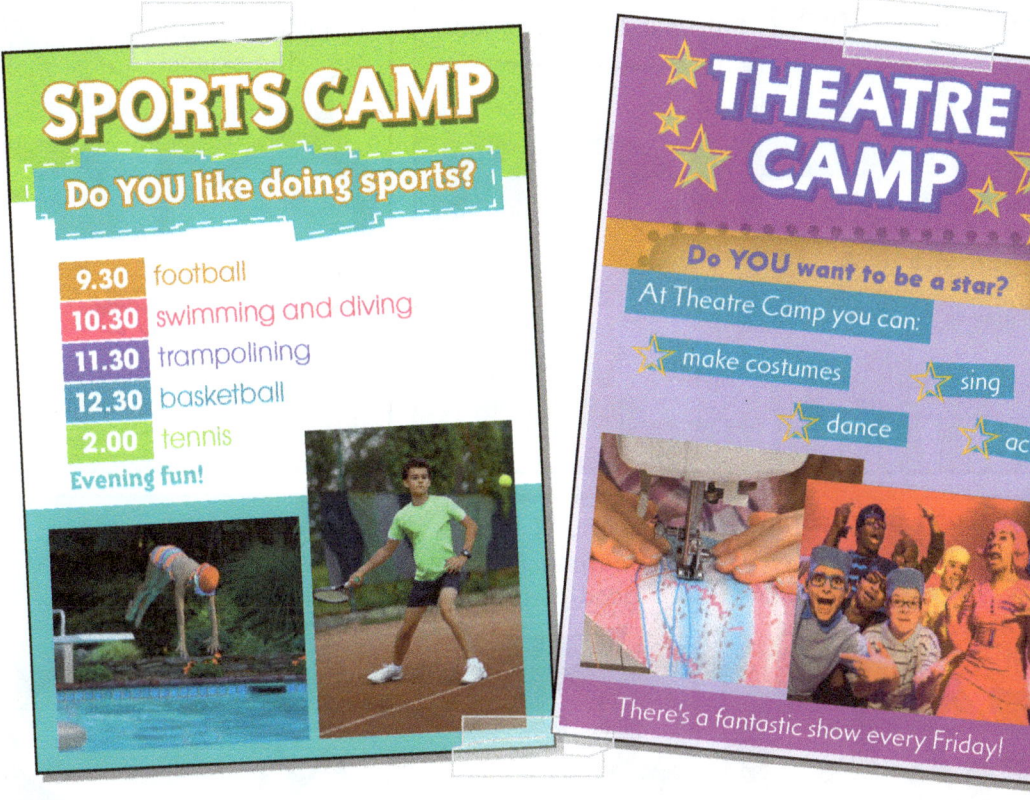

SPORTS CAMP

Do YOU like doing sports?

9.30	football
10.30	swimming and diving
11.30	trampolining
12.30	basketball
2.00	tennis

Evening fun!

THEATRE CAMP

Do YOU want to be a star?

At Theatre Camp you can:

★ make costumes   ★ sing
★ dance   ★ act

There's a fantastic show every Friday!

13 1:59 **Listen again. Then say.**

catching and hitting balls
playing basketball
running and diving
singing and acting
singing and dancing
throwing and catching

1 Hettie is good at ❓.
2 Hettie isn't good at ❓.
3 Cosmo loves ❓.
4 Cosmo isn't very good at ❓.
5 Fred likes ❓.
6 Fred isn't good at ❓.

SOUNDS FUN!

15  1:60 **Listen, read and say.**

I can dive and swim in the sea.
But he's good at **swimming** and
he likes **eating** me!

14 **Look and choose. Tell a friend.**

I like Sports Camp because I love diving and I'm good at playing tennis.

 STORY

BACK AT HOME

1 Eat your breakfast, kids.

2 Listen Mike. It's the skidoo!

Which way is it going?

3 Let's find those thieves! Come ON!

But I play football on Saturdays.

4 But I love football. And I'm good at football.

Well, you're good at finding thieves, too.

5 Is that the thief?

No, those are wolf tracks.

Rrrorf?

Look! A ribbon.

Let's go this way!

6 WOOF!

18 What do you know?

19 Read and say. *True* or *false*?

This is Harry Gregson-Williams. He writes music for films and computer games.

What films is your music in?
The *Shrek* films, the *Narnia* films and a lot of others.

You write music for computer games, too. Do you like playing computer games?
Computer games are OK but they aren't my favourite thing. I write my music on computers so I don't like playing on computers when I'm at home.

What instruments can you play?
I'm good at playing the piano and I can play the drums. I'm good at singing, too.

What's your favourite music?
Oh... I can't answer that question. I love listening to violins and trumpets but I love a lot of music!

1   He's good at playing the piano.
2   He can't sing.
3   He likes violin music.
4   He writes the stories for films.
5   He loves playing computer games.

20  Correct the false sentences in Activity 19. Say.

21  Listen to the music and number.

violins

drums

piano

trumpet

MINI PROJECT

22 Write interview questions.

- **Think** Do you know any musical people like Harry Gregson-Williams?

- **Plan** Choose one musical person and the things you want to know about him/her.

- **Write** Create five questions for a 'Discover a great musician' interview.

- **Share** Present your interview to the class with a friend.

HOME SCHOOL LINK

23 Listen and number. (First = 1, Second = 2.)

What are they doing?

1 Emma	2 Dan	3 Maddy	4 Mum and Dad
a	a	a	a
b	b	b	b

24 Unscramble and write sentences. Correct the false sentences.

1 playing / chess / Emma / likes

_____

2 good / football / at / Dan / is / playing

_____

3 is / drawing / at / Maddy / good

_____

4 like / mum / shopping / and / dad

_____

25 Think of an activity each person or pair likes doing. Write it down. Then ask and answer.

You	Your mum/dad	Your friend	Your brother/sister

Tom likes acting.

No. Guess again!

I CAN

I can talk about things I'm good at.

I can talk about things I like and love doing.

I can write interview questions for a musician.

26 Follow the lines. Find and unscramble the letters. Then write.

HAVE FUN

good at

loves

likes

1 Robbie _____. He _____, too.

2 Maddy _____. She _____ playing the _____, too.

3 Dan _____. He _____, too.

4 Emma _____. She _____, too.

27 What new things can they try? Give advice in pairs.

> Robbie, you like acting. You can try singing, too.

28 I want to know more!

Now go to Poptropica English World

Wider World 2
Funny sports

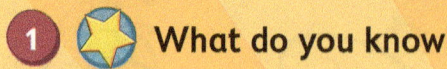

1  **What do you know?**

2  **Listen and read. What are the people doing?**

3 **Look and say.**

1 This is a sport with food.
2 This is a winter sport.
3 People run in these sports.

It's elephant polo!

1

Mud racing
Hi. I live in Scottsdale in the USA. In my town, there's a mud race every year. It's for children only. They can run, climb, swim and dive in mud. It's really funny. That's my brother in the photo. He loves mud!

Bianca, 11, the USA

2

Cheese rolling
Every May, people roll a big cheese down Cooper's Hill here in England. Then everyone runs down the hill. They want to catch the cheese. The winner can eat the cheese. My dad likes doing the race but he never wins. He isn't very good at running!

Freddy, 11, Britain

Can understand texts about funny sports

3

Reindeer racing
People love doing this sport in the winter here in Tromsø, Norway. The people don't ride the reindeer. They go on skis. The races are in the streets of the town and everyone shouts for their favourite reindeer. I love watching reindeer racing.

Ingrid, 11, Norway

4

Elephant polo
People usually play polo on horses but, here in India, people sometimes play polo on elephants. They sit on elephants and hit the ball with very long sticks. I don't play because I'm not good at hitting the ball. But I like watching.

Rajeev, 12, India

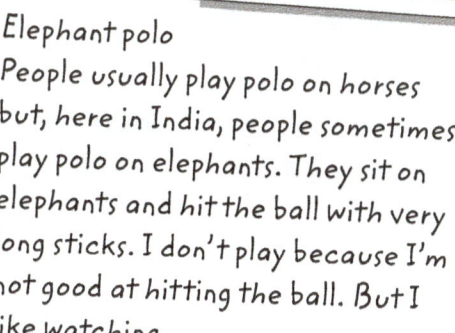

4  **Read again and choose. Tell a friend.**

A: I want to do cheese rolling.
B: Why?
A: Because I'm good at running and I love eating cheese!

YOUR TURN!

Talk about an unusual or funny sport in your country.

5 **Write.**

In our country, people love...

Can talk about funny or unusual sports

4 Around the world

1 **What do you know?**

2 **2:01 Listen and read. Does Dan like crocodiles?**

ROUND-THE-WORLD Holiday

COMPETITION

Dan: Look! There's a competition for a round-the-world holiday. The winner goes to Egypt and China, then Australia and Brazil.

Maddy: There are some beautiful beaches in Australia.

Dan: Cool!

Maddy: But, erm, Dan... there are a lot of crocodiles in Australia, too.

Dan: WHAT?!

Maddy: Poor Dan. Maybe you can have a holiday in Britain. There aren't any crocodiles here.

3 **2:02 Listen and say.**

1  Britain

2  Argentina

3  China

4  Mexico

5  Australia

6  the USA

7  Egypt

8  Spain

9  Italy

10  Brazil

4 **Which continent is your country in?**

> Africa   Asia   Australia   Europe
> North America   South America

Can identify countries and continents

5   **Listen, look and say.** *True or false?*

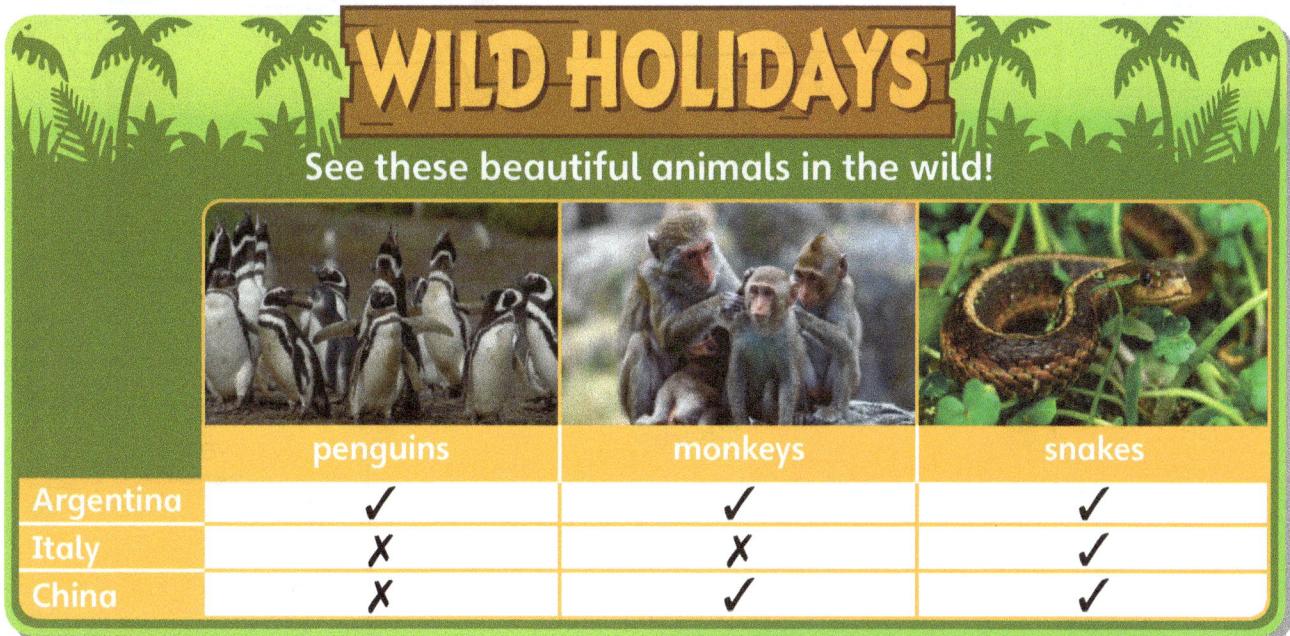

WILD HOLIDAYS

See these beautiful animals in the wild!

	penguins	monkeys	snakes
Argentina	✓	✓	✓
Italy	✗	✗	✓
China	✗	✓	✓

6  **Play the game.**

A: There aren't any penguins.
There aren't any monkeys.
There are some snakes.
B: It's Italy.

 **LOOK!**

There**'s a** competition.

There **isn't a** competition.

There **are some** snakes.

There **aren't any** snakes.

7   **Look and say.**

boat   dog   monkey   people   shark
in the sea   in the tree   on the beach

There's a dog on the beach. There aren't any people in the tree.

8 🎧 2:07 **Listen and say.**

1 forest

2 desert

3 pyramid

4 statue

5 city

6 cave

7 volcano

8 lake

Chorus:
The drums are calling. My home is calling.
I want to be there – in Mexico.

Tell me about your country.
I can tell you a lot.
Is there a desert?
Yes, there is. It's hot, hot, hot!

Chorus

Are there any volcanoes?
Yes, there are… and there are lakes,
Caves, forests and mountains.
It's a beautiful place.

Chorus

Are there any old cities?
Yes, there are. It's true.
With wonderful big pyramids
And statues, too.

Chorus

9 🎧 2:08 2:09 **Listen, read and sing. Does the singer like Mexico?**

10 🐛 **Look at the pictures. Ask and answer.**

- animals/in the desert
- island/in the lake
- statues/on the pyramid
- trees/in the forest
- volcano/in the city

A: Are there any animals in the desert?
B: No, there aren't.

🎧 2:10 **LOOK!**

Is there a desert?	Yes, there is. No, there isn't.
Are there any volcanoes?	Yes, there are. No, there aren't.

11 🐛 **Ask and answer about your country.**

A: Are there any deserts?
B: No, there aren't.

Can identify and talk about places of interest

12 Read. What's the name of the statue?

Dear Archie,
Hello from Egypt! It's very hot here but it's good fun. This postcard is from Giza. In the desert at Giza, there are some big pyramids and there's a big statue, too. It's called the Sphinx. It's got a man's head and a lion's body. It's very, very old. From Giza, you can see the city of Cairo.
Our hotel is on an island in the River Nile. There aren't any cars on the island. Everyone goes by boat. I can see some big white birds in the river.
This round-the-world holiday is fantastic! Are there any fun lessons at school this week?
See you soon,
Mia

Archie Joseph,
103 Park Street,
London, SE5 2XQ,
BRITAIN

13 Read again and say. *True* or *false*?

1 There are some big pyramids in the desert.
2 The Sphinx is a very old statue.
3 The Sphinx has got a lion's head.
4 Mia's hotel is on an island.
5 There are some hippos in the river.

14  Talk about where Mia can travel in your country.

A: Mia can go to Whitesea Island.
B: Why?
A: Because there are some good beaches.
B: OK. Let's choose Whitesea Island.

15  Listen, read and say.

Wh**ere**'s the b**ear** with spiky h**air**?
It's th**ere**, under your ch**air**!

1

Phew! What a climb!

The tracks are going north. Let's look at the map.

2

What's this place?

Hmm. Bollington Hall. Who lives there?

I don't know.

BOLLINGTON HALL

RESEARCH STATION

3

There aren't any roads to Bollington Hall.

MEANWHILE, AT BOLLINGTON HALL

4

There are some children in the forest.

Yes, boss. I think they're coming this way.

5

What?! Stop those kids!

Yes, boss.

6

Just get those kids away from here! They can't have the diamonds!

  Act out the story.

36 **Lesson 5**

Can understand a simple story / Can discuss a story

18 **What do you know?**

19 **2:18** **Read. Does Inuk like the summer or the winter?**

 **i-Blog**

Home | My favourites | Photos | Log out

My recent photos
Click here to read more

My recent posts

Hi. I'm Inuk. I live in Greenland. Winter and summer are very different here.

Winter

In the winter, we don't see the sun very much. There's one long night for four weeks in December and January. There are some big snowstorms and it's very, very cold. We go to school by skidoo because we can't use a car.

Summer

In the summer, there aren't any snowstorms. There are often long, sunny days. For a month, it's never nighttime! I go kayaking and fishing every day. The summer is great but it's very short. In September, it's time for my winter clothes again.

20  **Read again and say *summer* or *winter*.**

1 People use boats.
2 People use skidoos.
3 There are very long days.
4 There are big snowstorms.
5 There isn't very much sun.

21  **Talk about living in Greenland.**

A: I want to live in Greenland because I love the snow.
B: I don't want to live there. I love the sun.

MINI PROJECT

22 **Write a blog post.**

• **Think** about the summer and winter in your country. Are they very different? What months are the summer and winter?

• **Plan** by making a note of three things you like and three things you don't like about each season.

• **Write** a blog post. Include what you like and don't like about the summer/winter, what clothes you wear, how you get to school and what you do in each season.

• **Share** your blog with the class.

HOME SCHOOL LINK

23 2:20   **Listen and tick (✓).**

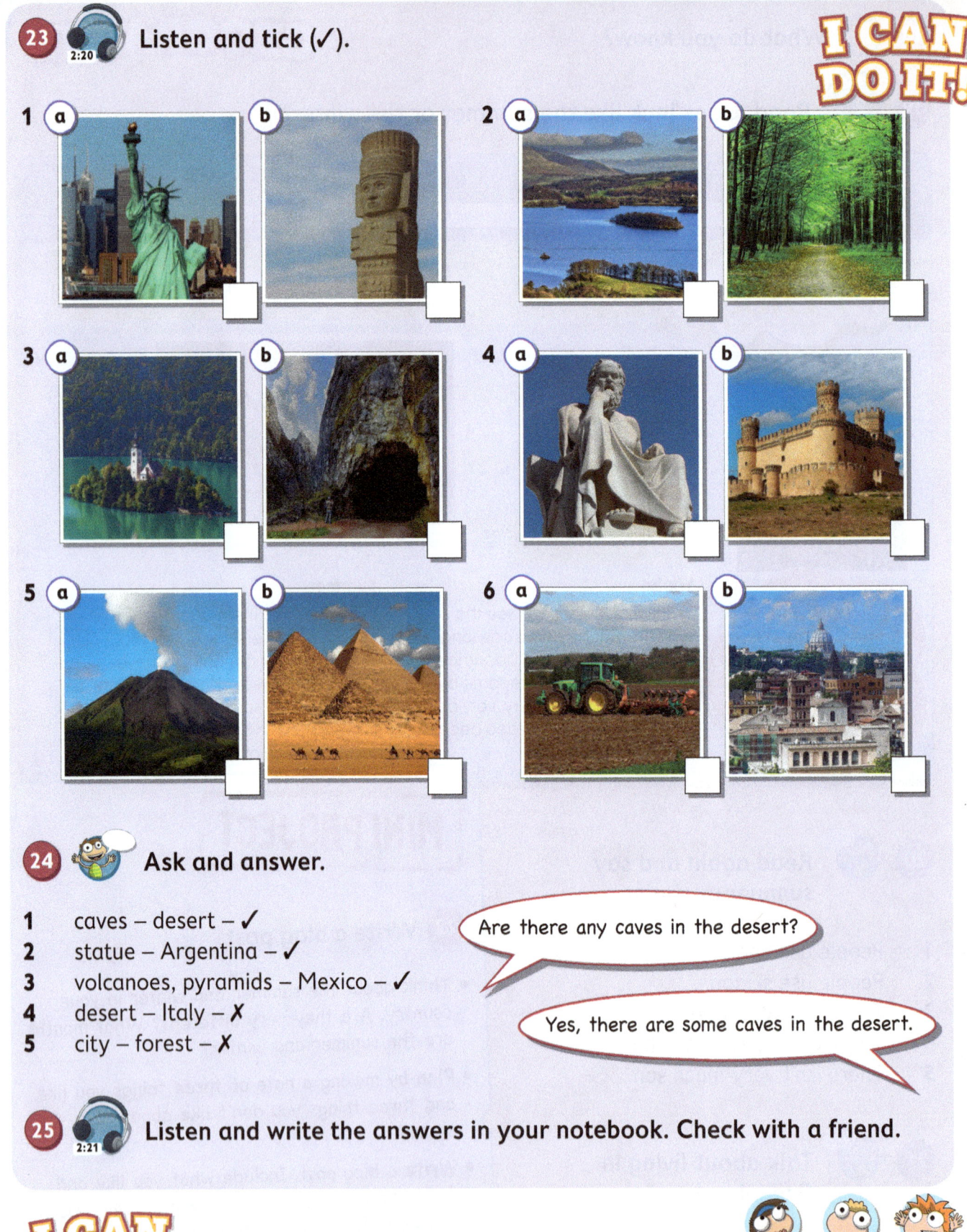

1 a   b

2 a   b

3 a   b

4 a   b

5 a   b

6 a   b

24   **Ask and answer.**

1   caves – desert – ✓
2   statue – Argentina – ✓
3   volcanoes, pyramids – Mexico – ✓
4   desert – Italy – ✗
5   city – forest – ✗

Are there any caves in the desert?

Yes, there are some caves in the desert.

25 2:21   **Listen and write the answers in your notebook. Check with a friend.**

I CAN

I can talk about countries and places.
I can ask and answer questions about my country.
I can write a blog post about seasons in my country.

26 Look at the pictures and circle the words in the puzzle.

M	C	D	E	S	E	R	T	X	C	A	V	E	K
E	M	W	V	T	V	G	Q	N	T	L	P	E	W
X	B	N	F	A	R	M	M	J	M	Y	T	B	R
I	V	C	X	T	Z	F	O	R	E	S	T	A	Z
C	M	S	D	U	F	G	H	J	R	K	L	Q	C
O	X	C	V	E	B	P	Y	T	E	R	C	W	H
N	L	M	S	D	F	G	H	J	T	K	I	L	I
Q	A	U	S	T	R	A	L	I	A	W	T	R	N
T	K	Y	P	Z	X	C	V	B	N	M	Y	S	A
D	E	F	V	O	L	C	A	N	O	G	H	J	K
Z	N	C	V	B	N	M	Q	W	R	T	Y	P	L

27 Unscramble the words and find the secret message.

1 There are pyramids and deserts.
EXOMCI
☐ ☐ ☐ ☐ ☐ ☐/☐ (6/7)

2 There's a very large rainforest.
RIZBAL
☐ ☐(11) ☐(9) ☐ ☐(12) ☐(1)

3 There are pandas and snakes.
NAICH
☐ ☐ ☐ ☐(8) ☐

4 There are beaches but there aren't any pyramids.
AASUTRIAL
☐ ☐ ☐(4) ☐(10) ☐ ☐ ☐ ☐ ☐

5 There's a very long river.
TEYGP
☐(2) ☐(5) ☐ ☐(13) ☐

6 There are castles and farms but there aren't any deserts.
RTIBIAN
☐ ☐ ☐ ☐(3) ☐ ☐ ☐

Secret Message = ☐(1) ☐(2) ☐(3)' ☐(4) ☐(5) ☐(6) ☐(7) ☐(8) ☐(9) ☐(10) ☐(11) ☐(12) ☐(13)!

28 I want to know more!

Now go to Poptropica English World

5 Shopping

1  **What do you know?**

2 🎧 2:25 **Listen and read. Does Emma buy the jacket?**

1. How much is that scarf?
   It's six pounds fifty.

2. And how much are those sunglasses?
   They're fifteen pounds.

3. Wow! I love that jacket and it's only twelve pounds.

4. Can I buy this jacket, please?
   £124.00
   Yes, of course. One hundred and twenty-four pounds, please.
   What?

3 🎧 2:26 **Listen and say.**

1.  jacket

2. scarf

3. swimsuit

4. wallet

5. sandals

6. gloves

7. sunglasses

8. umbrella

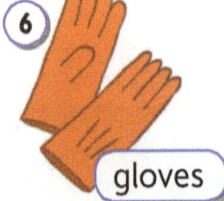

4 🎧 2:27 **Listen, look and say.**

Can identify clothing and accessories

5 Listen and repeat. Then look and say.

2:29

a £15

b £116

c £29

d £1000

e £2.50

f £360

g £12.50

h £28

i £18.50

6 Listen, look and say.

2:30

1 How much is that scarf?

It's two pounds fifty.

7 Look and invent prices. Then act out the dialogue.

A: How much is that pen?
B: It's three pounds fifty.
A: Can I buy the pen, please?

LOOK!

2:31

How much is that scarf?	**It's** two pounds fifty.
How much are those gloves?	**They're** fifteen pounds.
Can I buy this jacket, please?	Yes, of course. One hundred and twenty-four pounds, please.

a pen

b sweets

c guitar

d drums

e computer

f T-shirt

8  **Listen and say.**

1

2

tight trousers

baggy trousers

3

an expensive hat

4 £4

a cheap hat

5 £99

a light blue jumper

6

a dark blue jumper

9 **Listen, read and sing. What does the singer like wearing?**

That jacket's too short
And the colour's too light.
That hat's too expensive
And the size isn't right.

Chorus:
I only like wearing…
Baggy trousers, baggy trousers,
Baggy trousers, baggy trousers.
Baggy trousers are cheap,
Baggy trousers are cool.
Baggy trousers rule!

That jumper's too tight.
Those shorts are too long.
The shoes are too dark
And the size isn't right.

Chorus

LOOK!

2:37

It's **too** expensive.

They're **too** long.

10 **Look and say.**

Her sunglasses are too big.

- sunglasses/big
- jacket/tight
- trousers/short
- socks/baggy
- scarf/long

11 **Play the game. Spin, look and say.**

Three! Deserts are too hot.

1	tight	7	cold
2	cheap	8	big
3	hot	9	baggy
4	tired	10	shy
5	small	11	long
6	short	12	expensive

Can identify words that describe clothing and accessories

12 **Look. Are these stories, adverts or emails?**

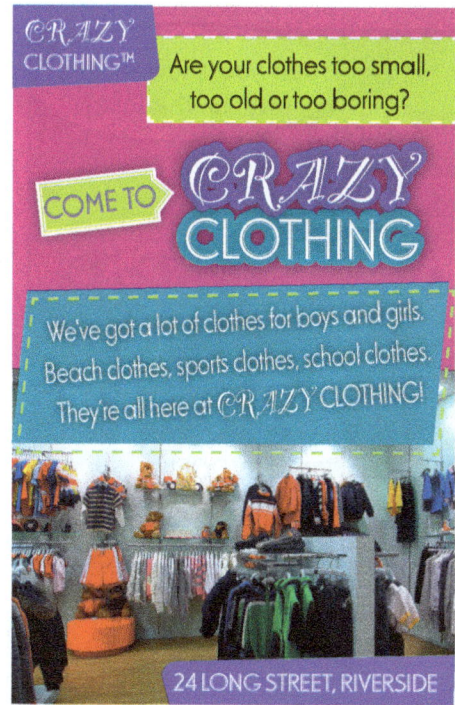

13  **You've got one minute. Read and say.**

1 Where can you buy toys?
2 Where is Crazy Clothing?
3 Where can you buy cheap trainers?
4 Can you buy food at Riverside Market on Sundays?
5 Can you buy gloves at Planet Sport?
6 Can men buy their clothes at Crazy Clothing?

SOUNDS FUN!

14  **Listen, read and say.**

I want l**ight** green pyjamas
for the n**ight**.
These aren't r**ight**.
They're wh**ite** and too t**ight**.

15   Talk about the pictures. Then listen and read.

2:42

STORY

1

How much is that jacket?

500 Ice pounds.

2

Can you show us the way to the lake?

Sure!

WOOF!

AT THE FROZEN LAKE

3

Wow! There are a lot of fish in this lake.

4

GRRR!

Are you OK?

Ye-e-s.

HELP!

5

OUCH! Get away from me!

GRRR!

Frost Inc.

SNAP!

6

Hey, Gizmo, what's this?

Come on. Let's get back to town.

Rrruff!

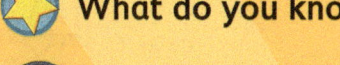
18 2:44 **Read. Then number.**

Choose the right shoes!

We all love wearing our favourite trainers. But for some activities, trainers aren't a good idea. Find out how to choose the right shoes.

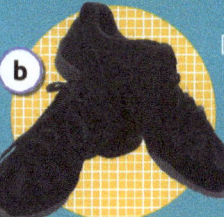

a In good weather, trainers are great for walking in a city. But on a rainy day, your feet get wet. Trainers are too soft for walking in the mountains. They can be dangerous. Always wear stiff walking shoes or boots.

c For rock climbing, you want to feel the rock with your feet. Trainers are too big for this. Climbing shoes are small and tight.

b Dancers move and bend their feet a lot. The trainers in this photo are good for dancers because the soles are soft in the middle. The soles of other trainers are too stiff.

What shoes do you wear for your favourite sport?

19  **Read again and say** *walking, rock climbing* **or** *dancing.*

1 You can't wear shoes with stiff soles.
2 Your feet bend a lot.
3 The right shoes are very tight.
4 Soft shoes can be dangerous.
5 Wet feet are sometimes a problem.

20  **Talk about the activities.**

A: I don't like rock climbing because it's too dangerous.
B: Really? I love rock climbing!

MINI PROJECT

21 **Design a pair of shoes.**

• **Think** about the shoes you've got. What are they for?

• **Plan** a perfect pair of shoes for an activity. Think about the soles, weight and what they are made of.

• **Write** about the shoes' features and why you chose them. Design and create a poster.

• **Share** your poster with the class.

HOME SCHOOL LINK

22 🎧 2:46　**Listen. Does she like a or b? Tick (✓).**

1　a　　b　　2　a　　b

3　a　　b　　4　a (£100)　　b (£60)

23 🎧 2:47　**Listen and number the three things they buy.**

a　　b　　c　　d　　e　　f

24 **Look at Activity 23. Use the key to ask and answer.**

Key:
1 = £95.50
2 = £62.30
3 = £22.99

How much are the yellow sunglasses?

They're sixty-two pounds thirty.

25 🎧 2:48　**Read and write. Then listen and match.**

a £65

b £17.50

c £12.50

d £85

1　How much _____ that jacket?
2　How much _____ those gloves?
3　How much is _____ swimsuit?
4　How much are _____ sandals?

I CAN

I can talk about how much things cost.
I can make sentences with *too*.
I can design a pair of shoes for an activity.

I CAN DO IT!

26 Play the game.

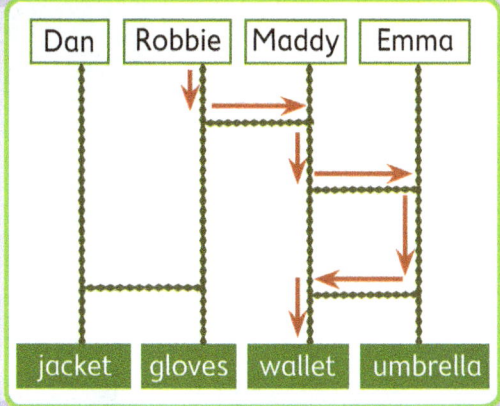

| Dan | Robbie | Maddy | Emma |
| jacket | gloves | wallet | umbrella |

Whose jacket is it?
It's _____.
Whose gloves are they?
They're _____.
Whose umbrella is it?
It's _____.
Whose wallet is it?
It's _____.

27 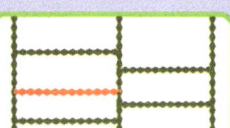 Play again and say. You can add extra lines to change the game. Add your own names for Number 4.

1

Dan Robbie Maddy Emma

guitar trousers computer sunglasses

2

Dan Robbie Maddy Emma

book trainers toy socks

3

scarf sandals T-shirt shoes

£12 £12 £10 £15

4

£1 £10 £100 £1,000

How much is that scarf?

It's ten pounds.

28 I want to know more!

Now go to Poptropica English World

Wider World 3
Shopping for food

1  **What do you know?**

2 **Look. Which foods do these people eat? Listen and check.**
2:52

1

Bao's blog

In Vietnam, we buy our food at the floating market. It opens at four o'clock in the morning. There are a lot of boats and you can climb from one boat to another to buy things. You can buy fish, rice, coconuts, bananas … and snakes, too! Some of the snakes can dance. I love watching them. Some people buy snakes for dinner but I don't eat snakes – they're too expensive.

Bao, 12, Vietnam

2

Silvia's blog

In Buenos Aires, Argentina, there are some amazing bakeries. You can buy a lot of different types of cakes there. There's a lot of *dulce de leche* or milk caramel in the cakes. I often go to a bakery after school with my friends. Cake is my favourite food.

Silvia, 11, Argentina

Can understand texts about shopping for food

Lily's blog

I live in Britain. My family doesn't buy fruit – we grow it in our garden. It's too cold for bananas but we've got a plum tree and two apple trees in our garden. In the spring and summer, we grow vegetables, too. There are some hens in the garden and we eat their eggs. They love eating our vegetable seeds!

Lily, 12, Britain

3 **Circle. Check with a friend.**

1 You can buy (snakes / cakes) at the floating market.
2 Silvia (always / often) goes to a bakery after school.
3 Lily gets her fruit from the (garden / supermarket).

4  **Listen and tick (✓). Who do you think said it?**

	1	2	3	4	5	6
Bao						
Silvia						
Lily						

5  **Ask and answer.**

1 Where does your family buy food?
2 Are there any markets in your town? What do they sell?
3 Do you grow any food at home?

6 **Write.**

My favourite place to buy food is…

YOUR TURN!

- Plan the food for a party with a friend.
- How many people are coming to the party?
- Make a shopping list and note where you can buy or find each food.
    Cake (bakery)
    Apple juice (supermarket)
    Strawberries (garden)
- Tell the class.

6 Party time

1 ⭐ What do you know?

2 🎧 2:54 Listen and read. Why is there a cake?

Yesterday was Grandad's birthday. All my aunts, uncles and cousins were at our house.

HAPPY BIRTHDAY GRANDAD

The cake was big but my baby cousin's cars were small.

There was a problem with the cooker.

Oh, no! We can't cook the food.

It's OK. We can eat Grandad's birthday cake.

Aarrgh!

I was very hungry yesterday.

3 🎧 2:55 Listen and say.

1 cousin
2 uncle
3 aunt
4 grandad
5 granny
6 parents
7 grandparents

4 🎧 2:56 Listen, think and say.

Can identify family members

5 **Read, look and say. Then listen and check.**

This is a photo of Aunt 's birthday. She was eleven. Those are her friends from school, ² and ³ . They were both ten. The young girl is your ⁴ – she was only five then. Those good-looking people are your ⁵ – yes, that's right, me and your granny. We were only thirty-five. And that baby with your granny is Uncle ⁶ . What a mess!

6  **Look and say.**

- Maddy's mum
- her grandparents
- her uncle
- her aunt
- her aunt's friends

> Maddy's mum was five.

 **LOOK!**

I **was** very hungry.
The cake **was** big.
The cars **were** small.
There **was** a problem.
There **were** some people.

7 **Play the game.**

> a pizza   a cake   children
> parents   pets   presents

A: There was a pizza at the party.
B: False.

8 **Talk about a party you were at.**

> There were twenty children.
> There was a big cake.

9 Listen and say.

1st first
2nd second
3rd third
4th fourth
5th fifth
6th sixth
7th seventh

8th eighth
9th ninth
10th tenth
11th eleventh
12th twelfth
13th thirteenth

14th fourteenth
15th fifteenth
16th sixteenth
17th seventeenth
18th eighteenth
19th nineteenth

20th twentieth
30th thirtieth

TIP!

twenty-**first**, twenty-**second**, twenty-**third**...
thirty-**first**, thirty-**second**, thirty-**third**...

10  Listen, read and sing.

It was the thirty-first of December, snowy and white.
I went to a party that cold winter's night.
There was singing and dancing, music and fun.
There were games. There were drinks for everyone.
I remember it well, oh yes, I remember it well.

Then... ten, nine, eight, seven, six, five, four, three,
two, one.
It was twelve o'clock! Another new year!

We said, 'Goodbye' to the old year.
We said, 'Hello' to the new.
My friends, new and old, said, 'Happy New Year!'
'Happy New Year!' I said, too.
I remember it well, oh yes, I remember it well.

11 Look and say. Use *I went* and *I said*.

 **LOOK!**

Hello   home   Goodbye   Thank you
to school   to bed

I **said**, 'Happy New Year!'
I **went** to a party.

12 Read. Was yesterday fun for Harry?

Sally's Welcome Party

Who? Sally's friends, classmates and teachers

Where? Standon School

When? Saturday, 18th April

What time? 6.30 – 9.00 p.m.

Harry's blog

Sunday, 19th April

Yesterday, we had a welcome party for Sally, a new pupil at school. Before the party, I went to my friend Mark's house for pizza. Then we went to school together in his dad's car. All our friends were there. Sally's parents were there, too. There was cool music but the room was too hot. There were some dancing games and a dancing competition. A lot of the girls were good at dancing and Mark was good, too. He was one of the winners. It was a fun night.

13  **Read again and choose.**

1 The party was at
   (school / Mark's house).

2 It was a party for
   (children / parents).

3 The party was on
   (Saturday / Sunday).

4 There was good (food / music)
   at the party.

5 There was a dancing (competition /
   show).

6 (Mark / Harry) was good at dancing.

14  **Imagine you are Mark.
Talk about the party.**

> Harry was at my house before the party.

SOUNDS FUN!

15  **Listen, read and say.**

Thanks for the **ph**oto of the **th**ree **th**irsty ele**ph**ants.

 STORY

1 Where are the kids?

Well, first there was a big wolf.

2 Then there was a huge polar bear!

3 It was too much! The kids just disappeared!

Really?

4 MEANWHILE, AT THE POLICE STATION

We've got this ribbon and this logo.

They belong to a thief!

I see.

5 Hmm. Hector Frost's got a dog and the dog's got ribbons like this. And this is Hector Frost's logo.

Wow!

6 Hector Frost lives at Bollington Hall. Come on, let's go.

  Act out the story.

Can understand a simple story / Can discuss a story

18 **What do you know?**

19 2:70 **Read. Then act out the mini-play in class.**

MINI-PLAY
The First Thanksgiving

In 1620, 102 settlers went from England to North America.

> Look at our ship. It's called the Mayflower. It was our home for many weeks.

> Now we've got a new home. But we haven't got food! And it's autumn! There is no time to grow food before the winter!

> I'm hungry.

> I'm scared!

The settlers' first winter in North America was very cold and snowy.

In the spring, some Native Americans went to see the settlers.

> You haven't got food. We are good at fishing and farming. We can help you.

> Thank you!

> Please teach us!

> It's autumn again. We've got a lot of food now.

The Native Americans were good teachers.

> We must remember to give thanks. Let's celebrate Thanksgiving every year!

20 **Circle T = *True* or F = *False*. Then correct the false sentences.**

1 The Mayflower was a ship. T / F
2 The settlers were from North America. T / F
3 Their first months in North America were fun. T / F
4 The Native Americans were good farmers. T / F
5 There was a lot of food at the first Thanksgiving. T / F

MINI PROJECT

21 **Write a mini-play.**

- **Think** What special celebrations do you have in your country?

- **Plan** Work in a group and choose one. Think about how you celebrate it. Find out about the history of this celebration.

- **Write** Write a mini-play about the history of this celebration.

- **Share** Act out your mini-play in class.

22 🎧 2:73 **Listen and number.**

23 🗨️ **Tell the story in Activity 22 to a friend.**

24 🎧 2:74 **Read and listen. Then write. Check your answers in pairs.**

I play basketball. My team is called Yellow Birds. On Saturday it was the last game of the season. Our team was first with **97** points. Brown Bears were second with **96** points. Blue Ducks were third with **80** points. Silver Snakes went up to fourth with **79** points. Red Cats were fifth with **78** points. Green Tigers were last in the league with only **70** points.

	TEAM NAME	POINTS	POSITION
1	Red Cats	78	
2	Green Tigers		
3	Brown Bears	96	2nd
4	Silver Snakes		
5	Yellow Birds		
6	Blue Ducks		

I CAN

I can use *was*, *were*, *went* and *said*.
I can use ordinal numbers.
I can write a mini-play.

25 Can you read the messages? Write.

CODE 1: DZ DZGS SV X MXLSC

1	2	3	4	5	6	7	8	9	10	11	12	13	14	15	16	17	18	19	20	21	22	23	24	25	26
A	B	C	D	E	F	G	H	I	J	K	L	M	N	O	P	Q	R	S	T	U	V	W	X	Y	Z
																					O				

Example: the twenty-second letter is really the fifteenth ➜ code letter V = O

The fourth letter is really the twenty-third.	The sixth letter is really the fourth.	The thirteenth letter is really the sixteenth.
The last letter is really the fifth.	The seventeenth letter is really the second.	The twelfth letter is really the eighteenth.
The seventh letter is really the fourteenth.	The first letter is really the ninth.	The nineteenth letter is really the twentieth.
The twenty-fourth letter is really the first.	The eleventh letter is really the seventh.	The third letter is really the twenty-fifth.

Message 1 = _____

CODE 2: UIFSF XBT DPPM NVTJD

1	2	3	4	5	6	7	8	9	10	11	12	13	14	15	16	17	18	19	20	21	22	23	24	25	26
A	B	C	D	E	F	G	H	I	J	K	L	M	N	O	P	Q	R	S	T	U	V	W	X	Y	Z

The second letter is the first.	The third letter is the second.	The fourth letter is the third and so on.

Message 2 = _____

26 Make your own code. Write a message to a friend.

1	2	3	4	5	6	7	8	9	10	11	12	13	14	15	16	17	18	19	20	21	22	23	24	25	26
A	B	C	D	E	F	G	H	I	J	K	L	M	N	O	P	Q	R	S	T	U	V	W	X	Y	Z

Code _____

Message _____

27 I want to know more!

Now go to Poptropica English World

School

1 **What do you know?**

2 **Listen and read. Why are Emma and Robbie scared?**

1. There was a story-writing competition at school today.

Were you the winner?

No, I wasn't. Stories are difficult.

2. Dan was the winner. His story, *The Green Hand*, was about a hand without a body.

Was it scary?

Yes, it was. The green hand went to people's houses and...

3. AAAARRRGGGH!

4. Ha, ha! Good joke, Dan!

Dan! That wasn't funny!

3  **Listen and say.**

 1 interesting

 2 boring

 3 exciting

 4 scary

 5 difficult

 6 easy

 7 funny

 8 relaxing

4 **Talk about these things.**

Snakes are scary.

- snakes
- playing football
- skateboarding
- holidays

- birthdays
- riding a bike
- books about monsters

Can use adjectives to describe experiences

5 **Listen and read. Then look and say.**

3:04

1 Were they exciting? Yes, they were.
2 Was it exciting? No, it wasn't.
3 Were there any children in it? No, there weren't.
4 Was there an alien in it? Yes, there was.

Story a and Story c.

Story Competition Winners

	Story a	Story b	Story c
	ISLAND ADVENTURE by James Duncan	**MIKE GOES TO MARS** by Isabella Brand	**Nile Princess** by Vinny da Souza
exciting	✓	✗	✓
scary	✓	✗	✗
funny	✗	✓	✗
children	✓	✓	✗
an alien	✗	✓	✗

 **6** **Listen, look and say.**

3:05

1 Was *Mike Goes to Mars* exciting?

No, it wasn't.

  7 **Play the guessing game.**

A: Was it exciting?
B: Yes, it was.
A: Were there any children in it?
B: Yes, there were.
A: It was *Island Adventure*.

 **LOOK!**

3:06

Was it scary?	Yes, it was. No, it wasn't.
Were they the winners?	Yes, they were. No, they weren't.
Was there an alien in it?	Yes, there was. No, there wasn't.
Were there any children in the story?	Yes, there were. No, there weren't.

8 3:07 **Listen and say.**

SONG

1

Maths

Chorus:
Maths, Science, History,
PE, Art, Geography.
A lot of subjects every day.
Is school boring? No way!

Last year, Maths wasn't easy.
The lessons weren't always fun.
But now I can do all my homework.
Maths is for everyone.

Chorus

Last year, PE was boring.
PE lessons weren't my thing.
But now it's my favourite subject.
I can play football and swim.

Chorus

2

Science

3 Art

4 Geography

5 PE

6 History

9 3:08 3:09 **Listen, read and sing.**

10 3:10 **Listen and read. Then look and say.**

These were my afternoon lessons last week.

Monday	Tuesday	Wednesday	Thursday	Friday
Maths	English	Geography	English	History
Art	Science	History	Science	English
Geography	Maths	Maths	PE	Maths

1 It was on Monday but it wasn't on Wednesday.

2 They were on Friday but they weren't on Monday.

3 It was on Wednesday but it wasn't on Friday.

4 They were on Thursday but they weren't on Friday.

LOOK!

3:11

Last year, Maths **wasn't** easy.

The lessons **weren't** fun.

11 **Play the game.**

A: PE was on Wednesday.
B: False. It wasn't on Wednesday.
It was on Thursday.

Can identify and describe school subjects

12 **Read. Then number.**

We love... SCHOOL TRIPS!

Where were you on your last school trip?

1 Our Science trip yesterday was exciting but scary, too. We went to a cave. In some places, there weren't any lights and the cave was very dark. There were a lot of bats. Yuk!

Oliver, 10, Birmingham

2 Last summer, our History lessons were about the Romans. My class went to some old Roman baths. They were really interesting. There were some funny people in Roman clothes, too!

Louisa, 10, Bristol

3 On Thursday, I wasn't at school. I was on a Geography trip at a lake in the hills. The river in my city starts at this lake. We went to a waterfall on the river, too. It wasn't very big but it was really beautiful.

Sam, 11, Leeds

a
b
c

---

13 **Read again and say. _True_ or _false_? Correct the false sentences.**

1 Oliver's Science trip was boring.
2 There were some funny people at the baths.
3 Sam and his class were in a city.
4 There was a waterfall on the river.
5 Louisa was on a Geography trip last summer.

> False. The Science trip wasn't boring. It was exciting but scary.

SOUNDS FUN!

14 **Listen, read and say.**

3:13

She ca**n't** sing but she does**n't** care.
It was**n't** a problem.
We were**n't** there.

EXIT   EXIT

IN THE FOREST

1. What's this place?

There's a tunnel in the caves. It goes to Bollington Hall.

2. It's a school timetable. How strange!

3. Oh! It's a school timetable!

It's a code.

Arf?

Science _ _ : _ _
Maths _ _ : _ _
Art _ _ : _ _

1 2 3 4 5 6 7 8 9 0

4. It's at nine o'clock. That's 09.00.

Quick, when's Science?

Maths is at 10.30 and Art's at 12.40.

Great! And Maths? And Art?

Science _ _ : _ _
Maths _ _ : _ _

3 4 5 6 7 8 9 0

5. Phew! We did it!

Awesome!

Great job, kids! Come on.

Science _ _
Maths _ _ : _ _
Art _ _ : _ _

1 2 3 4 5

3 -2

6. We're at Bollington Hall. Quiet now.

Look at all the lights! Are they having a party?

16   **Act out the story.**

Can understand a simple story / Can discuss a story

17 **What do you know?**

18 **3:18** **Read. Who were Tara's friends?**

Star Interview!

A lot of people know about your life as a film star in Hollywood. But where was your home when you were a child?

In the middle of the desert in Australia. It was 200 kilometres from other children and 500 kilometres from a city!

Was it very boring?

No, it wasn't. It was interesting. There were horses on our farm and a pet kangaroo. The animals were my friends.

Where was your school?

My lessons weren't in a school. My teacher was on a radio in the city and I was on a radio at home. There were other pupils on the radio, too and every year there was a big party in the city. I was shy with the other children but it was always a very exciting day.

Tara, 11

Tara, 14

Tara, today

19  **Ask and answer.**

1 Was Tara's first home in Hollywood?
2 Were there any animals on her farm?
3 Were her lessons in the city?
4 Was there a teacher?
5 Was there a party every month?
6 Were the parties exciting?

20  **Imagine you live in Tara's first home. Ask and answer.**

1 Is your life interesting?
2 Who are your friends?
3 What do you do every day?
4 Do you like your lessons? Why?/Why not?

 **MINI PROJECT**

21 **Compare your school life with your grandparents'.**

- **Think** about your grandparents' school lives. How do you think they were different to yours?

- **Plan** by making a note of six questions to ask your grandad or granny. Think about school subjects, teachers, classrooms and what pupils used (pens, books, computers).

- **Write** your questions and then interview your granny or grandad.

- **Share** your findings with the class.

HOME SCHOOL LINK

22 **Listen and write. Check your answers in pairs.**

I CAN DO IT!

	Monday	Tuesday	Wednesday	Thursday	Friday
1st lesson	(flasks)	(books ABC)		(books ABC)	
2nd lesson	English	(flasks)	(math)	(math)	
3rd lesson	(math)	(math)	(globe)		(math)
LUNCH					
4th lesson	(globe)		(art)	(music)	(art)
5th lesson	(history)			(sports)	

23  **Listen. Then ask and answer.**

> boring   exciting   funny   relaxing   scary
> Was it   Was there a   Were there any

Was it a funny story?

No, it wasn't.

24 **Unscramble to make questions and match. Then ask and answer.**

1 was / a / cave / there

_____

a Yes, there were. It was scary!

2 bats / any / there / were

_____

b Yes, there was. It was dark and wet.

3 boat / was / a / there

_____

c No, there wasn't.

 **I CAN**

I can describe things using adjectives and the past tense.
I can talk about school subjects in the past tense.
I can interview family members about their past.

25 **Find and circle seven school subjects. The letters that are left tell you the answer!**

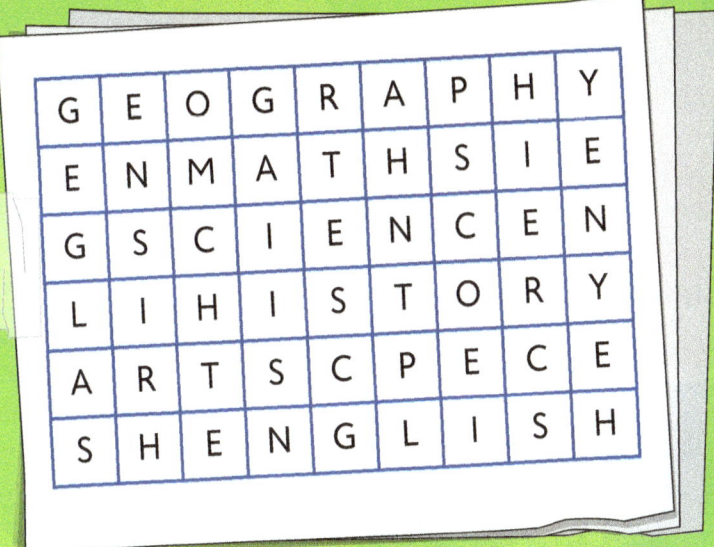

G	E	O	G	R	A	P	H	Y
E	N	M	A	T	H	S	I	E
G	S	C	I	E	N	C	E	N
L	I	H	I	S	T	O	R	Y
A	R	T	S	C	P	E	C	E
S	H	E	N	G	L	I	S	H

What are your favourite school subjects?

_____
_____

26 **How much do you know about what your older family members were like when they were younger? Take the test. Then ask and answer.**

Family member	I know! (score 2 points)	Score
1 For my _____,	school was (fun / boring).	
2 For my _____,	Maths (was / wasn't) easy.	
3 My _____	(was / wasn't) good at PE.	
4 For my _____,	_____ was relaxing.	
5 My _____'s	favourite food was _____.	
6 My _____'s	favourite film star was _____.	
7 My _____'s	favourite singer/band was _____.	

My total score	/14

10–14 Very good! You know a lot.   **5–9** Good! You know some things.
0–4 Find out more when you get home today.

27 ⭐ **I want to know more!**

Now go to Poptropica English World

Wider World 4
Unusual schools

1  What do you know?

2 🎧 3:24 Listen and read. Then number the photos.

a

b

c

1

Kai's blog

My new school in Tokyo is great. It's international so I've got friends from forty different countries! They always speak to me in English – their English is great. I'm learning Japanese. It was difficult at first but my friends were kind when I said the wrong words. Now it's easy.

Kai, 12, Japan

2

Abi's blog

I love my school! I go to a special school in the mountains. It's for pupils who want to study winter sports. Every day, after studying Geography, Maths and other subjects, we do sport for three hours. We go skiing and snowboarding. Some pupils from our school went to the Olympics. I want to be a famous skier, too.

Abi, 14, Canada

Can understand texts about unusual schools

3 Read and say.

1 Who lives in a school?
2 Who is learning Japanese?
3 Who does sport for three hours a day?
4 Who has got friends from forty countries?

4 Ask and answer.

1 Which school in Activity 2 do you want to go to?
2 What do you like about your school?

5 What is important about school for you? Tell a friend.

- good friends
- a swimming pool
- good teachers
- a lot of sports
- pupils from other countries

A swimming pool is important for me because I like swimming.

3

Matu's blog

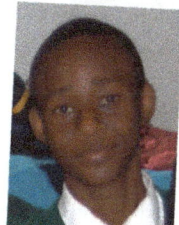

I live in my school because it's a boarding school. My friends and I all live in rooms next to the school. I love living with my friends and the teachers are all very nice. In the evening, there are a lot of activities. We can watch films or go swimming but usually we've got homework.

Matu, 12, Kenya

YOUR TURN!

- Think about your ideal school. How is it different from your school now?
- Make notes on your ideal school's subjects, sports, teachers and number of pupils.
- What else is special about your ideal school? *There is a rock climbing wall. / We watch a film once a week.*
- Tell the class.

6 Write.

At my ideal school...

8 Entertainment

1 What do you know?

2 Listen and read. Is Donaldo playing in the match?

Where's Donaldo?

Who's Donaldo?

He's a famous Mexican player. He was in an American team in 2007 and an Italian team last year. Now he plays here... but he isn't playing in this match.

Maybe he just isn't very good at playing football.

I am good! But look at my leg.

It's Donaldo! Can I have your autograph, please?

3  Listen and say.

1	Argentinian	**2**	Chinese	**3**	Italian	**4**	Spanish
5	American	**6**	Mexican	**7**	Brazilian	**8**	Australian
9	Egyptian	**10**	British				

4 Talk about famous people from different countries.

Lionel Messi is Argentinian.

Johnny Depp is American.

Can talk about different nationalities

5   **Listen and repeat the years. Then find and say.**

a — 1986

First, Kylie Minogue was an actress in Australian TV programmes.

b — 2001

Her song, *Can't Get You Out of My Head*, was very successful.

c — 2009

She was in the Indian film, *Blue*.

d — 1991

At the age of eight, Kaká was a young football player with a Brazilian team.

e — 2003

He was a new player in the Italian team, A.C. Milan.

f — 2010

He was in the Spanish team, Real Madrid.

6 **Read and say. Use *ago*.**

1 When was Kylie an actress on TV?
2 When was *Can't Get You Out of My Head* successful?
3 When was she in the Indian film, *Blue*?
4 When was Kaká eight?
5 When was he a new player at A.C. Milan?
6 When was he in a Spanish team?

LOOK!

She was in a film two days/months/years **ago**.

He was in a Spanish team **last** week/month/year.

7 **Play the game. Use *last* or *ago*.**

A: I was on TV last week.
B: False.

8 3:31 **Listen and say.**

9  3:32 3:33 **Listen, read and sing. What is the person's job?**

 **SONG**

On Friday, I was a cowboy.
On Thursday, a Spanish king.
In June, I was a waiter
And a sailor in the spring.

Chorus:
I'm an actor, yes, an actor.
Acting's the life for me.
I'm an actor, yes, an actor.
Acting's the life for me.

Last year, I was a scientist
And a soldier. That was great!
I was a famous British spy
In two thousand and eight.

Chorus

I get up at five in the morning.
My days are very long.
But a life in films is exciting.
That's why I'm singing this song.

Chorus

1 cowboy

2 king

3 waiter

4 scientist

5 spy

6 soldier

7 sailor

8 actor

3:34 **LOOK!**

| **in** the morning/June/the spring/2008 |
| **on** Thursday/16th January |
| **at** five o'clock/night |

10  **Look and say. Use in, on or at.**

> He was a waiter in June.

1 waiter / June
2 sailor / the spring
3 famous spy / 2008
4 king / Thursday
5 in bed / half past four
6 cowboy / Friday

11  **Ask and answer.**

1 Do you often watch films:
   a in the morning? **b** in the evening? **c** at night?
2 Do you often watch films:
   a on Wednesdays? **b** on Saturdays? **c** on Sundays?
3 Do you like films about:
   a spies? **b** soldiers? **c** cowboys?
4 Do you want to be:
   a an actor? **b** a scientist? **c** a waiter?

Can identify different occupations and use *in, on* and *at* correctly

12 **Read. Does the writer like the programmes?**

a **Big Kids**

Channel 1 at 6.00 p.m. on Tuesday, 28th June

In this Australian programme, children do their parents' jobs for a week and their parents go to school. This week, a boy is a waiter in an expensive restaurant and his dad has got some problems with his Maths homework. Very funny!

b **The Finton Files**

Channel 3 at 7.30 p.m. on Wednesday, 29th June

Harry Finton is a British spy in Italy seventy years ago. It's an exciting story and the actors are great.

c **Doctor Glock**

Channel 5 at 10.00 a.m. on Thursday, 30th June

A scientist and his alien pet go to the sea with some sailors. There are a lot of bad programmes for children in the morning but this one is fantastic.

d **The Big Match**

Channel 1 at 3.00 p.m. on Saturday, 2nd July

Barcelona play Real Madrid in the last match of the Spanish football season. Very exciting.

13  **Read again and say.**

Which programme:
1 is on Thursday?
2 is funny?
3 is at half past seven?
4 is in the morning?
5 has got sports people in it?

14  **Read again and choose. Tell a friend.**

> I want to watch *Doctor Glock*. It's fantastic.

 **SOUNDS FUN!**

15   **Listen, read and say.**

The swimm**er**s can't dance and the danc**er**s can't swim.
The sing**er**s can't act and the act**or**s can't sing.

1

THE QUEEN OF ICE ISLAND IS AT THE PARTY.

A dog costume – how interesting! And a police officer – how amusing!

2

IN THE ICE ROOM

Hello. I'm English.

Are you Italian?

I live on Mars. I'm a Martian.

3

Look! Do you see what I see?

Oh! The diamonds!

4

My diamonds! How extraordinary!

AARGH!

5

Quick! Catch them!

Those kids! I want to get those kids...

Help!

6

Excellent! You are brave and clever children. Thank you.

Just call on the Ice Detectives!

You're welcome, any time!

17 Act out the story.

Can understand a simple story / Can discuss a story

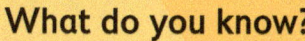

18 **What do you know?**

19 3:40 **Read. Then look and match.**

a

b

The history of computer games

Every year, there are new computer games. But let's look at some of the old ones...

1 The first computer games were American. Pong was new in **1972** and it was too big and expensive for people's homes. Two small white rectangles went up and down and a small white square went left and right. What was the game? Computer table tennis!

2 The Game Boy was Japanese. It was first in the shops in **1989**. It was small and there were a lot of good games for it. The games were black and white. Games with the character Mario were very successful.

3 The Wii was new in **2004**. In a lot of Wii games, you play with your whole body and not just your fingers. Some sports games are very good exercise!

c

PONG

ATARI

20 **Read again and say.**

1 Were the first computer games Japanese?
2 Was Pong cheap?
3 Were the first Game Boy games in colour?
4 Were the Mario games successful?
5 Was the Wii in shops five years ago?
6 Do you play some Wii games with your whole body?

21 **Talk about the computer games that you play.**

boring   difficult   easy   exciting   interesting

Do you play Wii games?

No, I don't. I think they're boring.

MINI PROJECT

22 **Write about a computer game.**

• **Think** about a computer game that you like. When was it new? Where was it made?

• **Plan** by making notes about how you play the game. Are there any characters? Is there a story?

• **Write** four or five sentences about the computer game.

• **Share** your paragraph with the class.

HOME SCHOOL LINK

23 Listen and number. Check in pairs.

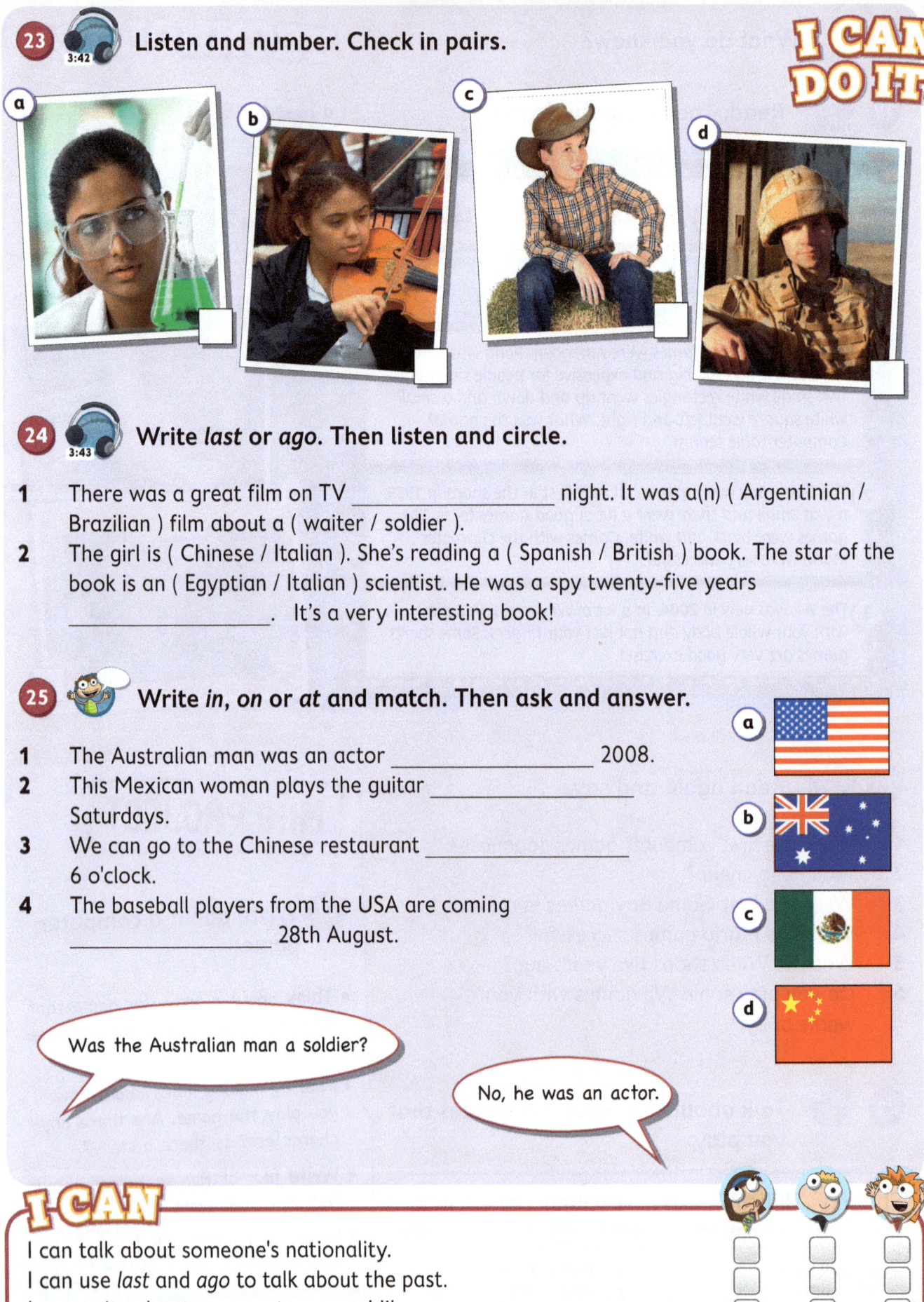

24 Write *last* or *ago*. Then listen and circle.

1   There was a great film on TV _____ night. It was a(n) (Argentinian / Brazilian) film about a (waiter / soldier).

2   The girl is (Chinese / Italian). She's reading a (Spanish / British) book. The star of the book is an (Egyptian / Italian) scientist. He was a spy twenty-five years _____.   It's a very interesting book!

25 Write *in*, *on* or *at* and match. Then ask and answer.

1   The Australian man was an actor _____ 2008.
2   This Mexican woman plays the guitar _____ Saturdays.
3   We can go to the Chinese restaurant _____ 6 o'clock.
4   The baseball players from the USA are coming _____ 28th August.

Was the Australian man a soldier?

No, he was an actor.

I CAN

I can talk about someone's nationality.
I can use *last* and *ago* to talk about the past.
I can write about a computer game I like.

1 Your film is...

exciting   funny   interesting   scary

2 Choose and describe three characters for your film.

actor   cowboy   king   sailor
scientist   soldier   spy   waiter

1   Country: _____   Name: _____
2   Country: _____   Name: _____
3   Country: _____   Name: _____

What do they look like?

1 _____
2 _____
3 _____

What are they good/bad at?

1 _____
2 _____
3 _____

3 What is your film about? Tell the class.

_____
_____
_____
_____
_____
_____

My film's very interesting. It's about a teacher. She loves reading. Her name is Rose and she's clever but very shy. She's got long black hair and green eyes. She's good at speaking other languages. She's Egyptian but everyone thinks she's Spanish. She helps an old explorer find treasure in the jungle.

27 ⭐ I want to know more!

Now go to Poptropica
English World

Goodbye

1 🎧 3:45 **Listen and number.**

2 🗣️ **Ask and answer.**

1 What was your favourite scene in the story? Why?
2 Who was your favourite character in the story? Why?
3 What was your favourite song in this book? Can you sing it?
4 Which 'Have Fun' page was the best in this book?

Can ask and answer questions about the story

3 Look and write. What unit are these pictures from?

1

Unit _____

2

Unit _____

3

Unit _____

4

Unit _____

5

Unit _____

4 Read and say. Who said it?

1 'Ah, those beautiful diamonds!'

2 'Eat your breakfast, kids.'

3 'This is a job for the Ice Detectives.'

4 'Then there was a huge polar bear.'

5 'A dog costume – how interesting!'

5 Read and say.

1 What's the name of the big house in the story?

2 What's the name of the bald thief?

3 Which thief loves diamonds?

4 What falls off a dog many times in the story?

5 Who wants to go to the lake?

6 Can Mike play football?

7 What does Gizmo look like?

8 Is Smith good at keeping fit?

9 What does Polly hear at night?

10 What is the code in the tunnel?

Grammar round-up

Unit 1

	do I	
What	do you	look like?
	does he/she/it	
	do we	
	do they	

I've got brown hair **and** brown eyes.
She's bossy **but** she's kind.
He doesn't talk **because** he's shy.

Unit 2

I brush **my** hair.
You tidy **your** room.
He makes **his** bed.
She meets **her** friends.
It washes **its** face.
We do **our** homework.
They brush **their** teeth.

Matt**'s** sister is pretty.
Sasha**'s** homework is very good.

Unit 3

I'm/I'm not		
You're/You aren't		
He's/He isn't		
She's/She isn't	good at	singing.
It's/It isn't		
We're/We aren't		
They're/They aren't		

What do you **like** doing?	I **like** acting and I **love** diving.
What **are** you **good at**?	I'm good at hitting a ball.

Unit 4

There**'s** a lake.
There **isn't** a forest.
There **are some** cities.
There **aren't any** statues.

Is there **a** statue?	Yes, there **is**. No, there **isn't**.
Are there **any** caves?	Yes, there **are**. No, there **aren't**.

Unit 5

How much is that jacket?	**It's** one thousand pounds!
How much are those gloves?	**They're** four pounds fifty.
Can I buy this swimsuit, please?	Yes, of course. Five pounds, please.

It**'s** They**'re**	**too**	expensive.

Unit 6

I **was** at a party.
You **were** happy.
He/She/It **was** great.
We **were** at school.
They **were** at the river.

There **was** a disco.
There **were** some people.

| I
You
He/She/It
We
They | **went** to a party. |
| | **said**, 'Hello.' |

1st	**first**	11th	**eleventh**	21st	**twenty-first**
2nd	**second**	12th	**twelfth**	22nd	**twenty-second**
3rd	**third**	13th	**thirteenth**	23rd	**twenty-third**
4th	**fourth**	14th	**fourteenth**	24th	**twenty-fourth**
5th	**fifth**	15th	**fifteenth**	25th	**twenty-fifth**
6th	**sixth**	16th	**sixteenth**	26th	**twenty-sixth**
7th	**seventh**	17th	**seventeenth**	27th	**twenty-seventh**
8th	**eighth**	18th	**eighteenth**	28th	**twenty-eighth**
9th	**ninth**	19th	**nineteenth**	29th	**twenty-ninth**
10th	**tenth**	20th	**twentieth**	30th	**thirtieth**
				31st	**thirty-first**

Unit 7

Was I at school?	Yes, you **were**.	No, you **weren't**.
Were you at home?	Yes, I **was**.	No, I **wasn't**.
Was he/she/it happy?	Yes, he/she/it **was**.	No, he/she/it **wasn't**.
Were we tired?	Yes, we **were**.	No, we **weren't**.
Were they funny?	Yes, they **were**.	No, they **weren't**.
Was there a cake?	Yes, there **was**.	No, there **wasn't**.
Were there any boys?	Yes, there **were**.	No, there **weren't**.

I **wasn't** at the party.
You **weren't** in the kitchen.
He/She/It **wasn't** scary.
We **weren't** on TV.
They **weren't** sad.

There **wasn't** a cat.
There **weren't** any dogs.

Unit 8

| **last** | week
month
year |

| | two days
six months
ten years | **ago** |

| **in** | January
the summer
1979 |

| **on** | Thursday
1st February |

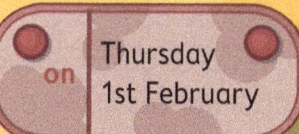

| **at** | night
half past eight |

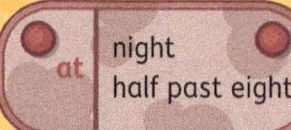

Thanksgiving

1  **Listen and read. What do people give thanks for at Thanksgiving?**

3:46

parade

trumpet

pumpkin pie

mashed potato

turkey

From: charlie@webmail.com
To: sarah@mail.com
Subject: Thanksgiving!

Hi, Sarah!

In the USA, we always have Thanksgiving on the fourth Thursday in November. It's a special day. We give thanks for our food. I don't go to school on Thursday or Friday. It's great.

On Thursday morning, there's a parade in the city. I play the trumpet in a marching band and the band is always in the parade. The parade is very noisy and colourful. I love it.

My family has a big meal at home in the afternoon. There's turkey and mashed potato, and then pumpkin pie. After the meal, we usually watch a game of football on TV – American football, of course. There are always a lot of good football games at Thanksgiving.

Tell me about festivals in your country.

Charlie

American football

2 **Read again and say.** *True* **or** *false*?

1 Thanksgiving is sometimes on Thursday but usually on Friday.
2 There's a colourful parade in the city.
3 Charlie dances in the parade.
4 Charlie's family has a big meal in the morning.
5 People can watch good football games on TV at Thanksgiving.

3 **Ask and answer.**

1 Is there a day of thanks for food in your country?
2 What is its name?
3 When is it?
4 How do you celebrate it?

Can talk about things relating to Thanksgiving